Money For Souls

Where do money for souls go?

Harvesting souls globally to use as miniature flying attacking beings.

David Gomadza

The First Global President of the World

www.twofuture.world

00447719210295

davidgomadza@hotmail.com

info@twofuture.world

PAPERBACK ISBN: 9798873193219

You must read Tomorrow's World Order

https://play.google.com/store/books/details/David_G
omadza_Tomorrow_s_World_Order?id=VDauDwAAQB
AJ&hl=en_GB&gl=US

You might want to read this book series as well.

https://play.google.com/store/books/series?id=a4MvG
wAAABBFmM&hl=en_GB&gl=US

VISIT

www.twofuture.world

DEDICATION

Changes.

6

TABLE OF CONTENTS

8

ACKNOWLEDGMENTS

Tomorrow's World Order

WHAT IS MONEY FOR SOULS

I need help
we are too many
who is this
Unknown1
what kind of help
any help damn it
you cursing sir do you know who ai am
what i care i just need help
help you came to the unknowngovernment1
this is unknown2 himself
unknown2 how are you
do you know me
maybe i know where money is going
ok i think that can interest me
so you help or not
let me get this straight what money
Money for the Souls
[surprised]
Money for the Soul
I only hear this but never been introduced
so tell more
when people die they leave everything but the money so where
do this money go
when people die they leave everything but the money
[heart-drop.soul.jumpout.searchforthemoney]
money goes to the unknwon3

ok

just to be sure you mean the unknown3of the unknowngovernment1 right?

yes unknown3 taking all money but unknown3 is not rich so where does all this money go

i want to know damn it

unknown1 that is a good question

i also want to know

unknown3 is poor so where does this money go

check

unknown3.poor.wheremoneygothen

check.end

start.end

[waiting for 2 minutes]

money goes to the unknown4 to the safe of unknown3

how

through moneyforsouls.received.unknown5

ok

check who is unknown5

why you ask

what do you mean

i mean you is unknown5

i am unknown5 how

all unknowngovernment1 leaders must send all moneyforsouls from everywhere of the unknown3 to moneyforsouls.received.unknown5

why is this money a secret

unknown3 tipofnose points to secret

check.unknown3tipofnose.start

your tipofnose has unknown3

can unknown3 hear me

yes

checking on you in case you decide to steal unknown2 like that $unknown1 from unknowngovernment2

safekeeping for unknown3

what can i do with this money then

[smile] what the fuck
you paid already for a unknown6 in uknown7 but great thinking
ok
the unknown6 must be in your name you mean
uknown2 are you still there its unknown1
ok i am still here
so how can i help you
you have a message unknown2 [trust me something like this has never happened-thinking]
press the tipofnose
with any finger
fingerprint check
unknown2 confirmed
keep the money you wanted to use it for campaigning for that you are closer to me right
yes unknown3 thank you
from today now you know where to send this money ok
moneyforsouls.received.unknown5
[thinking]
do i just say send money to moneyforsouls.received.unknown5
yes and give it to unknown4
which unknown4
unknown7 branch send it there in unknown8 and say unknown3 send me and must be sent to moneyforsouls.received.uknown5
ok unknown3
sign out end.now
[thinking]
unknown1
deadline
damn it
i want unknown1 get him
ask your brain it will tell you
what
just say last contact.who
ok
last contact.who

saved as uknown1.unknowngovernment3
press where i showed you
press there and say unknown1.unknowngovernment3 can we talk
ok
uknown1.uknowngovernment3 can we talk
who is this its unknown2
[do i keep pressing whispering]
no once is enough we can do the rest
unknown2 [pause] how did you contact me
I ask you the same question
i just said i need help with people who can help me with removing too many souls
ok
what did you say [wondering]
call unknown1.uknowngovernment3
ok i didn't even know
how then did you do all this so i know its trusted sources
uknown3.souls
did you touch anywhere else
tipofnose
so unknown3 can hear you
unknown3 can hear me good what i care i need help help help
i cant pay for anything
if this goes on like this we are finished
i have no job at all
who can go back on to what they were doing after becoming unknown10
[thinking]
[unknwon2 surprised]
let me get this straight
you want help to save your soul
why you talk about the soul unknown2?
is my soul at risk?
what are you talking about
[too tired]

ok
i need help stop asking me boring questions [laugh]

is that a punch line
maybe bitch eeh what can i say
[angrily]
do you know who i am
[silence]
i think you are a coward you rather sacrifice women and
pensioners to keep up with things
just wait until things start not balancing from your side ok that's
ok unknown2 don't ever call this way again
what if
do you know that the brain will forever keep this record what if
someone smarter like Yahweh can read this
[a laugh]
no one in our generation will ever become so smart like Yahweh
to read this file I must say first time as well i have been through all
this

[**David Gomadza has risen to the top and can read the brain
and has decoded the brain and act just like Yahweh - i have
Yahweh's image see this link
https://x.com/DGomadza/status/1722707319178334642?s=20
Ladies and gentlemen welcome to Tomorrow's World Order a new
world order we know everything visit www.twofuture.world]

so you know a lot about this
Yahweh the mighty God is how he read your brain he will know
everything you did this way but only Yahweh no man in billion years
will ever be like Yahweh for real that I guarantee you so we are safe
then
i can say that uknown3 is now hearing us
[pause and whispers]
[unknown1 speaking] he said that unknown3 is listening right
now

check [asking another person]
how
close your eyes and say
check.anyunknown3listening.start
nothing
check again make sure you put correct question just know I might have made a mistake
[thinking if i make a mistake can the message go]
message is not in a spoken language no
the brain compose electromagnetic waves that match meaning and send that with a seal in most cases the seal is the message so that it is easy to unlock when message is read the seal is received and used to dissipate the message as well
yes something inside me said yes unknown3 is listening
[cursing]
dropping down in seat
what is the problem
we cant receive anything unknown3 is the one who put us in this position in the first place
if she is listening that means just putting our place in a worse situation
[signaling- knife on throat]
unknown3 stole everything we had in the name of unknown9
[angry]
why
unknown3 wants unknowngovernment4 in all her banks
what
how can unknown3 get unknowngovernment4's money
do you know how much
[ask just to prove and show]
ask say
unknowngovernment4.inuknown3land.start
pause followed by silence
$unknown4
say in uknown3currency.start
pause

$unknown2

it must be more than that

it is actually $unknown3

deflate and seat

that means uknown3 might not need anymore once unknown3 get this

[thinking]

uknown2 calling [uknown1 brain]

we need an answer fast uknown2

ok leave this with me i will talk to unknown3

ask unknown3 what is her commission because we are doing this to raise more money from the world

[uknown2] uknown1 is either stupid or suicidal there is no other explanation

that's the advantage of the uknown11 you can do anything and cover it up i do not think you can do the same in the unknown12 you shit your pants just thinking about stealing $uknown1 uknown2

[bust of laughter from uknown1]

so you been checking on me

just checking if we can use something against you in the future to shut your ass tight not literally unknown2

[another burst of laughter]

i am not gay its called doing unknown3 uknowncommands1

[another laughter]

check your things moving already but I just want you to know that I am married and have a wife who I love very much so I am off boundaries i do not want any special attention like you gave to [thinking]

what was his name again

silence

[feeling angry]

then i cannot help you because if this comes out i am destroyed not just me but him too

who is he what is his name again

unknown1 looking in the air [top of the building]

i know you like then uknownpeople1 but just know

unknownpeople2 are not unknownpeople1 so stay away from me

[pause - sexual arousal]

i will make this clear if you talk about my private life I will kill you okay

that is exactly what I am saying unknown2 [agitated]

have you been at the unknowninstitution1 its the land of the free and what happens there stays there

hey i did not ask you to do that did he

i lied that unknown3 was listening

what

silence

i am listening [unknown3]

unknown2 surprised

but i am not pressing the tipofnose [uknown2]

i know but i am [unknown1]

uknown1 [tired]

why not sleep over this but remember even uknown3 cannot reveal this or else even uknown3 is gone

unknwon3 is listening unknown2

how is uknown3

what is that supposed to mean

i have not sleep for 8 days i haven't showed or_ was to say fuck my wife

why not do her while I do unknown3

[laugh]

unknown2 uknown3 cannot have a grip at the same time

thinking what that meant

unknown1

so you agree right we are in together

but what i get

silence

you must ask the commission so we decide how to do this

i know what unknown3 wants

what is that what unknown3 want

75%

unknown3 will not waste resources for less and just to make this clear I will need 50% of what is left after unknown3 has taken share

unkown1 surprised

unknown2 are you out of your mind only unknown3 can take money for the souls

unknown2 thinking

but unknown3 can take $unknown6 unknowngovernment4 money

how much did you say

$unknown3 `

that is what i am talking about and not money from the soul

[changing first reference of money from moneyofthesouls to unknowngovernment4's money]

you said money already in unknowngovernment1

[pause thinking]

why can't we exchange you get money from donations then we just get some of the unknowngovernment4 this will be faster don't you think

thinking

you must be Yahweh to do that because only you can prove all this

but one question how does this Yahweh do it to know everyone's thoughts i wish someone out there get to know all this so that i expose you for who you are a unknownpeople2 in every meaning of the word

aggravated you mean killing women and pensioners is not for money and is in honor?

silence

[he got me -whispering]

how then you want this resolving

ok i make it easy for you

10% of unknowngovernment4's money is mine

[unknown2] but you claim it then when i come then give all to me in a bulletproof jacket

ok

thinking [unknown1]
you want only 10% [thinking]
i thought you were going for 25%
so when they kill you you know why they are killing you

surprisingly, you were saved on my ribs [dick throbbing]
unknown1 opening his mouth
hey i don't do that shit unknown2 i have a wife unknown15 men
will never understand the bond between a man and a woman i
promised i never look for another you should see how she looks

you said you haven't fucked her for unknowndays1
i can go there right now
huge feelings of rage
for what he paused and looked at someone
moneyforthesoul moneyforthesoul-lost-love
what lost soul I mean soul-what
he said moneyforthesoul-lost-love
someone explain what he is trying to say

whispering he is saying that he can get you killed and give the
money to your wife as compensation or insurance life policy
unknown as if thinking but something holding him inside a face
clamp source [uknown3]
hurry up my dick is throbbing [no throbbing dictated -by the
brain {added}]
how much you said anywhere
silence
35% and [tongue between teeth and wriggling]
thinking
same feelings as before
i will think about it [uknown1]
he might want to kill her then what will i be doing all this for i
told her i can kill anyone for you
[cursing] siting down i was just joking
unknown2 you lie to me and I fucken kill you myself you what I

can put a bomb in the money jacket and a GPS tracker to see where you will go with money and go and get it
   [unknown2 smiling] did you check what's in your tipofnose now
   unknown1 asking
   how can i check
   [unknown2 thinking] did it go through
   [unknown1] touching tipofnose
   something just arrived
   unknown1 looked lost] they can easily insert things all of them and why no one here know how to do this and you call yourselves educated than unknown1
   instead of unknown3 think about me [unknown2 smiling]
   you replaced unknown3
   [unknown1 thinking]
   yes you deal just with me they are stealing anyway to make things worse killing innocent women and children maybe its time for unknown3 instead
   silence

   so its you not unknown3 killing these people in the first place unknown2 i am here because people are being killed by this knocking his back and only those with money and the money is drawn and it disappears from uknowngovernment3 so i ask you are you the one killing us in the first place
   i have to check and get back to you
   i want 50% if its you killing them compensation will cost you an extra 35% [pause]
   is it why you only asked for 10% [pause] [unknown2 thinking]
   unknown1 clever you are if you are this clever why not use it to get all the money you need
   you know what forget about all this i don't care
   ok ok ok 35% of only unknowngovernment4's money for you the rest must be given to unknowngovernment3
   all countries on earth must give us money to rebuild
   our problems solved i get to fulfill my wish to my beautiful [who sits me down with love]

ok the conversation has been too long we don't want Yahweh to think that I am testing him
unknown1 surprised
did he say Yahweh [looked surprised]
ok sleep over it
`

MANIPULATION OF DNA SEQUENCE EMBEDDING CODES THAT MAKE PEOPLE KILL WOMEN AND CHILDREN AROUND THE WORLD

Some regimes are manipulating DNA sequences to influence how people react when faced with certain situations.

2876 whenatwarpaymoney.start

GGAAAATTGGGG for men.

2180 wheninvadedreceivemoney.start

CCTTGGAAGGGG for men.

620 whenatwarwomenarecollateral.start

CCAATTAAGGGG for men

632 whenatwardontthinkaboutwomenandchildren.start
CCGGAATTCCGG

778 whenatwardon'tnegotiate.start

CCGGTTAAGGGG.

They have created DNA sequences that they have embedded inside people that makes people for example instead of negotiating for peace instead refuse [778] and fight to death with the hope of receiving money since everyone has a DNA sequence that tells them that when someone is invaded [2180] he must receive money and if that country is at war then others have to pay money [2876].

These regimes need only to say the code to command the brain of the person in question for him to do what the DNA sequence code means. Often this is in terms of money.

Someone from the regime only needs to send money or other items like weapons but in exact code numbers that match the DNA sequences. For example, if a leader is at war there can be times that he does not even make love to his wife. The regime can take his wife and give her to one of them and give her 600 dollars and all the woman has to say is that someone from this regime gave me 600 dollars. On hearing this number, the body activates DNA sequence 600.

600 whenatwargiveyourwomantoothers.start

The man now knows why this is happening normally where the woman goes for a long time, making the man agitated enough to start a fight with her. Hearing this code will calm him down.

It is like when a leader at war is about to negotiate for peace with the enemy. The regime who wants the war to prolong will simply give anything in amount that matches the DNA sequence code that forbids negotiations.

778 whenatwardon'tnegotiate.start CCGGTTAAGGGG.

When at war don't negotiate

To us as Tomorrow's World Order the codes, we are against the most are codes 620 and code 632 that allows the disregard to women and children during war commanding these men through DNA sequence manipulation to disregard the lives of women and children and consider them as collateral.

Code 620 whenatwarwomenarecollateral.start

CCAATTAAGGGG for men

When at war women are collateral .start

632 whenatwardontthinkaboutwomenandchildren.start
CCGGAATTCCGG

When at war don't think about women and children .start

689
whenapersonhasdiedmoneygotomoneyforsouls.received.uknown5.start

The code that is a hinge-pin to this book is the code 689 of any DNA sequence. This code is the one that puts a risk to anyone because this DNA sequence code says when a person dies money go to moneyforsoul.received.uknown5.start

When a person dies this code tells those who are left where the money should go.

That means the regime behind all these codes can easily monitor money in everyone's bank account by a simple DNA sequence code.

A spying device can easily be installed on anything and even you and then DNA sequence is used to tell the brain to check the amount in the bank and whisper this to the hearing device that then sends a message to the regime.

DNA sequence 628

Checkbankbalanceandwhispertome.start

GGTTAATTCCGGG

Check bank balance and whisper to me .start

This DNA sequence will tell you anyone's bank balance.

The regime can easily check everyone's bank balances and know you they call cash cows [stable revenue sources] people who are rich with money and life insurance. These people are targeted until death. DNA sequence to kill is.

Code 7285

Killstartkillstartkillstartkillstart.start

Kill start kill start kill start kill start .start

Once the code has been initiated then the person one way or the other will end up dead.

Once he has died then code 689 is also triggered

Whenapersonhasdiedmoneygotomoneyforsouls.received.uknown5. start

After this code then code 781 is triggered as well

When[lifeinsurance money is received]moneyforsouls.received.unknown5.start

This code gives commands regarding the person's life insurance money. If this money is received it must be sent to moneyforsouls.received.uknown5.start.

As you can see a regime can easily select the rich or those with life insurances that can pay and trigger the domino effect that can culminate with the person's death and his or her life insurance money being sent to the regime.

All this is happening through a simple DNA sequence code.

Now in the next chapter I will explain how this is happening in real life. In other words, one can ask how do they do this? Are you saying they say codes all the time and the body simply obeys?

17

HARVESTING OF SOULS THEY ARE USING AS DNA SEQUENCE CODES TO GIVE INSTRUCTIONS TO HUMAN BODIES.

The regime is getting people killed mainly women and children wherever it starts wars and harvest souls literally from the dead bodies. They resurrect these souls, the electromagnetic wave entities which are the real person, the ones that think, talk, and make body functions. These don't die forever but can be dissipated by a triangle. See my other books.

They then bring all these to their country and give them passports and actually tell them. These are given mainly numbers that start with 72 and the number is a twelve-digit number.

They then give these little fairies numbers and instructions promising them rights and that they will become humans one day. These fairies [little devils] are told that to become humans they must invade a human body and cause fatal injuries acting like diseases like cancer etc. For them they are eager to become human and hope to take the human body of their victims when he dies. So, they become so dedicated to causing injuries and harm to the body. In the hope that they become humans as they are the critical part of thinking of a human being.

A human being has three things critical to life, thinking and memories.

1. This electromagnetic wave is the person responsible for thinking and conveying messages. Converting electromagnetic waves to voice and vice versa. This knows everything and has

your memories. This is the entity that has memory of yourself since birth and above all contributes to the recovery and reading of this memory.

This on death remains in the body.

2. The soul that goes to Yahweh.

3. You.

Now what they are doing is get people killed and harvest these electromagnetic waves of humans and instruct them to act as weapons, diseases etc embedded with instructions to kill and cause grievous bodily harm. They can now after harvesting easily clone these to millions and use these as weapons. They are real people they fly and can do anything it is instructed to do. Very clever and all with goals to take the body after death. These are now the new weapons that people must fear.

The real beings killing people globally.

Therefore, wars do not necessarily mean regime change but harvesting for them.

Once the war is over these are then sent back to these countries with DNA sequence instructions embedded inside them and are used to help this regime to clone everyone.

Once they have your clone, they simply give your clone instructions and send your clone to you. Since it's your clone your body will not reject it and will simply let it in. It will go inside you without you noticing.

If instruction is to make you buy or do something e.g., take life insurance if you didn't have it. Then automatically you will then get life insurance.

Ever had a situation when you don't want something, and you feel like something runs inside you in a flash then all of a sudden you want to do something you didn't even think about before?

But in worst case scenarios when there are no wars and they have used all stock or running low on stocks they remove these from living people and swap with their own who can attack you .

They use code 728.

attackasinstructed.start

GGGGGGGGAAGGG

Attack as instructed.

To believe us just say 728 if you have any of these, they will start attacking you but don't worry we have a code to stop these.

GGAAGGAAGGGGG

For a man first say.

"My voice is my password."

GGAAGGAAGGGGG

Space out.

End.

Out.

Space In

Start.End

Permanent save.

THE LACK OF MONEY TO PAY FOR SALARIES ETC MONEY TAKEN BY THE REGIME AS MONEYFORSOULS IS THE TRIGGER OF THE INITIAL PROBLEMS.

What I want you to ask yourself is this. Why do these wars start?

In the scenario above. Unkown1 ran out of money. All the wealthy people and those with life insurance were dying and the money they had that could have been left for the relatives was disappearing .

Uknown1 asks.

".when people die, they leave everything, but the money so where does this money go?"

The regime is creaming everyone globally, killing relentlessly for

money in banks using code 628 and 678 and code 679.
    DNA Sequence code 678
    Checkvalueoflifeinsurance.start
    GGAATTAAGGGGG
    679 ifvaluableaboveUS$1millioninform.me.start
    GGAATTAACTCTGGG

In the scenario above the deaths of people and the disappearing of the money worsened unknown1's situation that he starts asking for help.
    i need help help help.
    i can't pay for anything.
    If this goes on like this we are finished.
    ...
    I just said I need help from people who can help me with removing too many souls.

Unknown1 is in a tight place he can't pay for anything, money for the rich and those with life insurance are disappearing fast. Those who pay taxes and capital gains taxes etc. Now unknown1 can't pay dependencies like women and children on benefits, the pensioners and even the soldiers. What can he do?
Now he is left to ask for compensation from the regime who have stolen the money.
But outright he knows why the regime is doing this. The killings and extraction of the money is to put him in a position where he has to sacrifice women and children, pensioners, and dependents as well as soldiers.
They are all deadwood and must be eliminated if you want to afford to pay.
Unknown1 now is in a position where he has no option, they have already initiated the moneyforsouls by killing the rich and those with life insurances. Now only what unknown1 can do is to ask for money for the souls in his brain thinking compensation at least 10% from the money already taken.
But the regime has bigger plans for him, that's why they put him in

such a position.

Why not get all these deadwoods killed and get even better money for the souls from around the world.

Around the world?

Yes, all you must do is trigger a war.

Put conditions that upset unknowngovernment4 to such an extent that they will invade. They invade we activate code 2180 wheninavdedreceivemoney.start

When invaded, receive money .start to make sure that every nation on earth will give you money. Secondly, we will activate code 2876 that commands every nation on earth to pay money when a nation is at war.

That means unknown1 will in the end bulge in to pressures to start a war or do something that will contribute to initiating a war.

FOREIGN MONEY IN UNKNOWNGOVERNT1'S BANKS AS INCENTIVE TO HARVEST SOULS AND MONEY ABROAD WITH HOPE OF GETTING ALL THIS FOREIGN MONEY.

The main reason why the regime is doing this is the fact that foreign money in local banks has risen sharply, mainly above $US20 million to make any move lucrative. The regime can easily check using DNA Sequences embedded in everyone globally.
Code 1028
Checkforteignmoneyincountrybanks.start
GGAATTAATTGGG

Code 1029
InformifinvestmentmoneyisaboveUS$20million.start

If the country has enough foreign money in its banks it simply gets messages informing it how much is in the banks. They initiate the harvesting of souls from local people in the country. They want to start a war with a country dumping most of the money which they call dirty money. Stolen from a corrupt government. This regime considers that it has the right to take all this money as it is stolen money. Even if some are not.

The regime will now offer some of this money to the country in question. This will be used to entice the country into doing things that will start the war. This is because the money is immediately available. The country is offered a percentage of the money which can be delivered fast once the war has started because the country must tell the entire world to confiscate money of the invading country and give it to them.

Money from those who pay money to the invaded country will now go to the regime. This is because the invaded country will have been given a share of the frozen money of the invading country as a cash advancement.

All frozen money assets in other countries will be sent to the regime as moneyforsouls.received.unknown5

THE TRICK QUESTION OF ALL THIS IS THE FACT THAT THE REGIME IS POOR CONSIDERING THE MONEYFORSOULS BEING HARVESTED THAT LEAVES EVERYONE ASKING: WHERE DO THE MONEY FOR THE SOULS GO?

The regime by modern standards is regarded as poor as compared to its status. The money harvested globally does not tally with the wealth the regime has. So, the question that is in everyone's mouth is where does the money for the soul go?

Does the regime hide the money somewhere and where?

Are there others involved in all this?

Are we looking at a vast network of soul harvesting and money "laundering"?

Where does the money go? We all know it is a fact that there is some harvesting going on. We all at one point have been victims and we want to know.

Where do the money for the souls go?

WHERE DO THE MONEY FOR THE SOULS GO?

Who controls the world's money?

If the thieving, murdering and money laundering regime is broke as well, so tell me where does all this money go?

Who else can possibly be involved?

But unknown1 called for help.

All the unknowngovernment1 did was offer help. Shouldn't we be thanking the cleverness of unknowngovernment1?

But then again unknown1 only called for help because money was disappearing from his country.

Yes, but what does that money have to do with paying for salaries and dependents benefits and pension incomes? Maybe the regime actually helped this unknown1 by showing him the real help he needs.

Culling all dependents and deadwood. This is the kind he needs the real help he needs. So don't blame the regime. The regime is performing a critical function and works at commission. Even if the commission is high, you asked for help it's not the other way round.

Unknown1 [imaginary not real]

Sits down says.

Damn it. They steal from us so that we ask them for help and in the end, they just give us the money they stole from us, above all asking us to pay the interest on top of that.

Not only that after looting not just our money but our souls even of the living ones now they want us to get loans from them so that we sink deeper in debt.

Can someone out there help?

Anybody apart from these bloody thirst corrupt people in the world.

Do we have someone not corrupted by all this?

Someone fresh like Tomorrow's World Order.

Because all these are crooks.

They first robbed me.

They removed all souls so that we can't fight back.

They killed everyone rich and took all the money.

They are still killing and creaming all the money out of the country.

The only reason I called for help is to find out who is doing this.

If I find him or her then ask him or her what he wants and why he is creaming us financially and soul as well.

To my shock I am telling the truth someone has targeted us just because of the vast foreign wealth now in their country.

We only get a 15% commission and all the money we will raise from the war which I am reluctant to start will all go to them.

What is 35% to 50% of pity money?

I had suggested 75% of the money in their country ready and waiting to be taken.

I need real help to deal with these because it is them who put us in this position in the first place.

Please help.

Anybody?

He sobs and sits down.

The world is not a fair place.

I am calling all you thieving bastards to stop existing if harvesting money and souls is all you can do.

Anyone out there who can stand for justice like David Gomadza and his Tomorrow's World Order.

All this money they are stealing from us will be offered to us as loans.

Just imagine our own money, now we must pay exorbitant interests on top of something that was stolen from us.

But why?

Hey, you asked for help. You came to us not us coming to you.

Do not be a smart ass. You stole from us and killed and harvested our souls even for those alive living in a state that they cannot fight you. Now you want to offer us loans at unaffordable prices. Our own money you have been stealing over the years.

No, I refused.

I think if everyone else is like you then they all must stop existing.

We can simply say you want to be a macho man, a hero and it is you getting people killed.

But who started killing us first?

Was it not you?

Where can you get free money? Even us where do you think we can get this money from.

All these people you cry for were just keeping money. That is why you were having money problems. We take all this money tied up in banks and life insurance policies. Now we will give you back the money and pay us for teaching you how to deal with money shortages.

It is not that you do not have the money. It is because a few of you keep the money from everyone else.

For our advice you must pay interest of 12 to as high as 40% on any borrowed money.

One condition is that you must kill all women and children. The DNA Sequence inside you will make you do what we want.

DNA Sequence 620 will make sure that you do what is right given the circumstances. The money we are going to give you is to pay for productive uses only. Things that give you some money back. That means all deadwood must be burnt. If you cannot do it, we will let unknowngovernment4 do it for you.

But how?

How and how did you contact us?

I accidentally touched my tipofnose.

He will touch the tipofnose as well.

I do not get it.

For him his reasons are genuine, he will fight for his people. Do defend them as he has lost his people.

Someone revenging like that will not give a toss about your women and children. If you can do to him what can stop him from doing the same to yours.

I can tell you that all your problems have been solved.

All deadwood is gone, and we give you all your money back, but you must pay us interest for the advice and keep your people streamlined as such. You start breeding like dogs then we will be back.

How much loan do you need?

Loan? But how can we pay for a loan?

We want our money back.

No chance you must pay interest as all the people we took this money from have died and their bodies have commanded the living relatives where the money goes?

But how? They were all already dead. When the money was released.

Their bodies obey us and give everyone commands just like a will does their will which we must obey.

Are you tampering with people's DNA Sequence for your own benefit?

We have a problem.

[Call from far away.] What problem. Do not talk nonsense. You know the code.

What code?

799.

799 [speaking in the face of unknown1]

Okay I will obey.

What?

Check what does code 799 do?

DNA Sequence 799

Obeyanddoasaskedby [unknown3representative].start

Obey and do as asked by [unknown3representative].start

Unknown1 sits down.

But who are you?
The man walks to the door and stops at the door.
We are …

Loan sharks and we keep all the Money-For-The-Souls
…
The real owners of the money act poor but they come for it privately here and there and take it as cash in black bags.
We are just the keepers of the MoneyForTheSouls
Any more question you want to ask?
…
Silence
[pondering]
How do you live with yourself..
Killing women and children
…
All my men have died for nothing
..
But we offer a service which you can either take or deny. It is that simple.
Simple?
After creaming us killing everyone leaving us on our knees above all take all the souls even of the living?
Somebody has to do it its either us or someone else?
How much is in the MoneyForTheSouls Account?

US$2 billion

A gun shot rocketed in the skies.

Don't shot!
We can put your son in power and see if he can do better? But let me warn you if he asks us for help. We are going to blast him. He better keep his finances straight. But on one condition.
What is that?
We all walk free and consider all the loans as written off.

David got up and looked lost.

My son? But my son is only 8 years old.

How can you complain and point fingers at us if your son is the one in power?

The only way for him to be in power is for you to die first.

Unknown20 pulled the gun fast but David had anticipated this.

Seven gun shots rocketed into the skies.

I will put a new system that is fair and where people earn their monies and where no one is robbed. Nor where a single soul is lost or removed.

Above all where there is no Moneyforthesouls.stillunknown5

A new voice message has just been received

Anyonewantsmoneyforthesoulofunknown20.received.start

[any one wants money for the soul of unknown20.received.start]

I don't want his money.

But you killed him you are entitled to his money? Said a soul that came out of the message.

Just joking. There is no money.

His money has already been sent to Moneyfordirtysouls.received.unknown5

So what do you want?

Silence and a cheeky grin.

His body. I can be human again you know.

The soul flew to the dead body.

Oh my God did you have to shot him that much. I guess the body is useless. I could have given him a good brain to think straight and not ask for money for the souls all the time.

Silence.

Do you know they removed me from my body when I was still alive.

Literally kicked me out of my own body and replaced me with their own soul and kidnapped me bringing me here all the way from Kabul, Afghanistan?

What [softly and shocked]

Ok you don't care.

Money for The Souls! Anyone. [shouted the soul flying away]

What?

The soul suddenly stopped flying.

What am I saying. [the soul asking itself]

I retract that. I meant anyone with a body he does not need?

Help help help! I need a body can someone help me?

The soul suddenly stopped and flew back.

Honestly did you have to shot him that many times?

If you knew the amount of money he collected as money for the souls then you would understand.

It is genocide. I mean holocaust!

What is holocaust?

But I thought you said that they took your soul while you were alive. That means you must know all these things.

The souls flew closer to him.

They wiped everything but I had already saved my memories. Keep this.

What is it?

A shining stone but not just a shining stone all my memories are inside it.

He looked in his hand and suddenly the souls disappeared the second he looked in his hand.

I want your body I can wait. [he heard a whispering voice]

Get out right now!

Don't shoot I can tell you where the Money-For-Souls-Go but you have to help me find a body.

Tell me first where the Money for the souls go?

If money found then return the soul.

If Money Found

Then return the soul?

The soul suddenly fell to the ground and vanished.

A beep went off from his pager. The message read.

Souldissipated.Moneyreceived.start

If Money Found

Dissipate The Soul

THE END.

33

Money For Souls Moneyforsouls.received.uknown3

ABOUT DAVID GOMADZA

I am the first global president of the world.
Visit www.twofuture.world
00447719210295
davidgomadza@hotmail.com
info@twofuture.world

36

www.ingramcontent.com/pod-product-compliance
Lightning Source LLC
Chambersburg PA
CBHW051400250726
48656CB00006B/2189